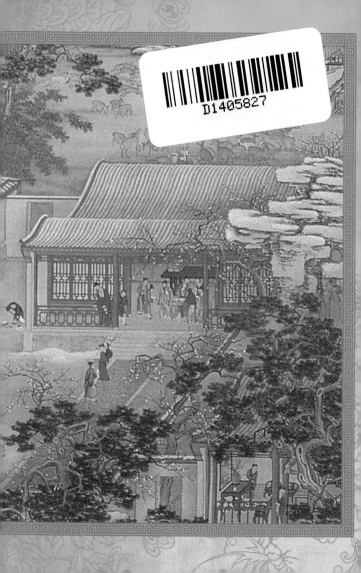

KUAN YIN

觀
音

KUAN YIN

Divine Giver of Compassion

TEXT BY Manuela Dunn Mascetti
DESIGN BY Bullet Liongson

Manufactured in China
Typeset in Copperplate and Goudy Oldstyle
ISBN 0-8118-4105-7

10 9 8 7 6 5 4 3 2 1

Distributed in Canada by
RAINCOAST BOOKS
9050 Shaughnessy Street
Vancouver, BC V6P 6E5

CHRONICLE BOOKS LLC
85 Second Street
San Francisco, CA 94105
www.chroniclebooks.com

観音

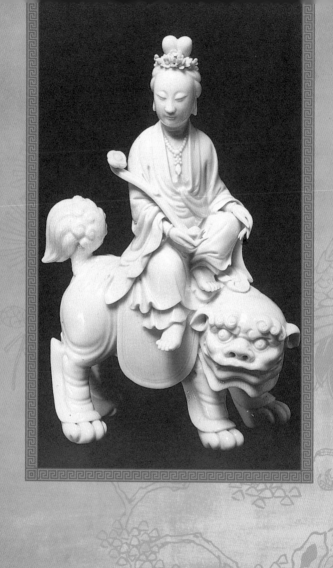

Table of Contents

觀
音

Introduction

Kuan Yin is perhaps the most important and best-loved enlightened being in the Chinese world. She is a *bodhisattva*, an individual who after her enlightenment has taken an oath to postpone her own final bliss until she has helped every other creature become enlightened. Only then will she be able to depart the worldly realm and become a deity dwelling in the heavens. Kuan Yin's oath ties her to humanity: She is the very special being who answers prayers, petitions, and cries for help, who comes to the rescue of those in need or in danger. She is a friend, intercessor, creator, and a living incarnation of infinite compassion, and these qualities have made her the most widely worshiped bodhisattva in a large part of Asia.

She often appears as a gracious lady, her rounded cheeks and chin as smooth as porcelain, and is sometimes depicted sitting quite informally upon a throne that looks like a rock, one of her knees raised up so high that the elegant slipper peeping from beneath her robe is on a level with the other knee, just as in the statuette you find in this box.

Her temples in China, Japan, Vietnam, and Korea are often situated beside rivers or along the seashore, in pleasant spots on the outskirts of towns and villages. They appear wherever her followers have traveled, including the United States. Most frequently they are women's temples, where small groups of girlfriends will stop on their way to or from work to make offerings to the Bodhisattva, asking for help, offering prayers, and lighting candles and incense sticks. Until recently, little was known in the West of Kuan Yin's history, origins, or miraculous works. Asian immigrants have now brought their favorite goddess to their host countries, and her presence has entered the lives of many people on other continents. More and more, her likeness is found in the United States and Europe—in Chinese shops and Buddhist temples, in Asian art galleries, sitting peacefully by gardens and fountains inspired by Chinese principles and design, or simply as a sacred image displayed on the wall in one's home.

觀音

The Kuan Yin box is a miniature temple to the Bodhisattva, and the book you are reading explores the history, qualities, and nature of Kuan Yin. The figurine included is an elegant and popular representation of her. Traditionally, figures of Kuan Yin are worshiped in Buddhist temples, but due to her immense popularity, they can also be found

on home altars, in meditation corners, on scholars' desks, by bedside tables, or in sacred gardens.

Kuan Yin embodies the Divine Feminine, an exquisite essence whose chief attribute is pure, unwavering compassion. She is unique in the heavenly hierarchy in being as free as a buddha from pride or vengefulness and is ever reluctant to punish even those who might deserve it. In her infinite compassion, Kuan Yin protects all good people and grants all positive wishes.

As the "Compassionate One," Kuan Yin is deeply engaged in the day-to-day world of men and women. She is sensitive to the ordinary situations anyone might face, and when called upon, she intervenes with divine aid. Not removed like a buddha, Kuan Yin represents the tangible aspects of compassion, love, hope, transformation, and service.

觀
音

She is revered by men, children, laywomen, and Buddhist nuns, and in this respect bears some resemblance to the Virgin Mary or the Jewish *Shekinah*, the Goddess of Mercy. The Bodhisattva will come if you call her, chant her name, place flowers on her temple, or meditate by her statue. She will cure your illness, grant you a child, save you from disaster, and lessen your sorrow. As an object of spiritual worship, Kuan Yin helps devotees transform themselves, and for meditators she provides a fluid, feminine, powerful guidance along the path. Buddhist men and women may honor any bodhisattva they like; for centuries Kuan Yin has been one of the most beloved.

The Chinese Bodhisattva of Compassion

Every evil state of existence,
hells and ghosts and animals,
sorrows of birth, age, disease, death,
all will thus be ended for him.
True Regard, serene Regard,
far-reaching, wise Regard,
Regard for pity, Regard compassionate,
ever longed for, ever looked for
in radiance ever pure and serene!
Wisdom's sun, destroying darkness,
subduer of woes, of storm, of fire,
illuminator of the world!
Law of pity, thunder quivering,
compassion wondrous as a great cloud,
pouring spiritual rain like nectar,
quenching all the flames of distress!

—THE LOTUS SUTRA[1]

觀
音

In China, Kuan Yin's name means "she who hearkens to the cries of the world," for she takes human form in order to comfort human beings and rescue them from disaster. As a bodhisattva, Kuan Yin is holier than a mere deity, for Buddhism makes distinctions between buddhas, bodhisattvas, and deities. *Buddha,* for instance, is a title rather than a name; translated literally, it means "the awakened one," referring to someone who through his or her efforts and concentration has attained enlightenment. A buddha is considered the highest being in the universe, higher even than the gods, who are often represented in humble positions, paying homage and listening to the teachings of a buddha. The Indian prince Gautam Siddhartha is called "the Buddha," because on attaining enlightenment he brought his wisdom to millions of disciples, revolutionizing the religious path to the ascended state. But there are many other buddhas who are venerated and bless life with their light.

The term bodhisattva is composed of *bodhi,* meaning "the state of being awake," and *sattva,* meaning "mind" or "intention," thus a *bodhisattva* is one whose mind or intention is directed toward enlightenment. The ideal of the bodhisattva arose within *Mahayana,* one of the two main forms of Buddhism. *Theravada,* meaning "Teaching of the Elders," focuses on a strict understanding of the teachings of the historical Buddha. On this path the individual struggles toward enlightenment for many lifetimes, reborn as successively higher beings.

Mahayana, which means "Great Vehicle," offers the possibility of release from the cycle of birth, death, and rebirth through the help of holy and pure individuals—bodhisattvas. Through spiritual practice, anyone may become a bodhisattva, whether a monk, nun, or simple layperson. One who attains this state embodies infinite wisdom and compassion: This is the being who has taken a vow before ten thousand buddhas that he or she renounces ultimate bliss until the task of helping every other sentient being to become enlightened has been completed.

Kuan Yin thus serves her worshipers in two manners: She grants wishes to those in need, out of her compassion to bring light into the world, and in meditation she reminds us by her gracious example of the powers that reside within each of us to manifest buddhahood.

The passage that opens this chapter is taken from the Lotus Sutra, composed in Sanskrit in the first century C.E. and later adopted as one of the main sacred texts of Chinese Pure Land Buddhism, a school of Mahayana. Like Christianity, Buddhism has many sects and schools, and Pure Land thought and practice emphasize faith in one's capacity to achieve buddhahood; Kuan Yin is one of its central figures. Amitabha Buddha, perhaps the most popular buddha in China, presides over the Pure Land—a "paradise" believed to be in the West—

a land of ultimate bliss. The Pure Land is free from the suffering, defilement, and delusion that blocks people's efforts toward enlightenment here in our world. The immediate goal of Pure Land believers is to be reborn in Amitabha's paradise. There, in more favorable surroundings and in the presence of Amitabha, they will eventually attain complete enlightenment.

The Lotus Sutra heralds the coming of Avalokitesvara, "the lord who regards the cries of the world," a being who has lived lives of such pure and exemplary quality as to have eliminated his own karma, and who has built up an immense store of spiritual merit with which he can free all life from the struggle of birth and death. Delaying his own final enlightenment, Avalokitesvara hears the cries of the world and helps all other beings to be released from the wheel of birth, death, and rebirth and the constant suffering it entails.

Avalokitesvara was the object of a major cult following from the beginning of Buddhism in India in the early centuries of the Common Era until its disappearance from Southeast Asia in the twelfth century. Subsequently Avalokitesvara was accepted and worshiped in other Buddhist countries: China, Java, and Tibet. The Lotus Sutra was one of the first sacred scriptures to be translated into Chinese. The Chinese translation of the bodhisattva Avalokitesvara's

name is Kuan Shin Yin, "the one who hears the cries of the world," though it is popularly abbreviated as Kuan Yin, the name used in this book. Thus from the very beginning, Avalokitesvara was worshiped in China under a name evoking the same attributes as his Sanskrit one. Though originally a male figure, Kuan Shin Yin was always portrayed as almost androgynous or genderless, gracefully sitting with one leg bent, his hand relaxing on his knee, and dressed in flouncing robes.

This passage in the Lotus Sutra recounts the moment when the Buddha entrusts to Kuan Shin Yin the role of savior for humanity:

The Buddha told the Bodhisattva, "...If sentient beings encounter hundreds, thousands, or millions of difficulties and disasters and their sufferings are unlimited, they will be delivered right away when they hear the name of Kuan-shin-yin and be freed from all pain. ...If someone keeps his name in his heart and falls into a fire which rages through hills and fields, burning forests, shrubs and houses, the fire will immediately die down when he hears the name of Kuan-shin-yin. If a person enters into a river and becomes frightened because of the swift current, when he calls the name of Kuan-shin-yin and takes refuge in him single-mindedly, the authority and the supernatural power of the bodhisattva will protect him from drowning and enable

*him to reach safety. When a person sails in the ocean with
many people to obtain pearls, corals, amber, etc., and
the boat carrying the treasure enters a whirlpool and is
about to be sunk by a sea monster, if he secretly thinks
about the bodhisattva's majestic power and calls his name,
then he and his companions will be saved. ...The realm of
Kuan-shin-yin is without limit because it has his authority,
supernatural power and merit. Because he is full of
illuminating light ["kuan" in Chinese], he is therefore
called Kuan-shin-yin."*

—THE LOTUS SUTRA[2]

Regarded as a universal savior, Kuan Shin Yin
became extremely popular in his new land and soon
had his own Chinese cult following. Stories were
written about him, and his image began to appear
in Buddhist paintings.

THE NEED FOR A FEMALE BODHISATTVA
In the chapter of the Lotus Sutra foretelling the
Bodhisattva's coming, the sacred scripture states that
Kuan Yin can appear in as many as 33 different forms
in order to succor different kinds of devotees. Seven
of these forms are feminine: nun, laywoman, wife of
an elder, wife of a householder, wife of an official, wife
of a Brahmin, and simply a girl.[3] In other scriptures,

Kuan Yin also appears as a princess, queen, noble lady, or virgin.

The need for a female Buddhist figure arose both within the monasteries and among the laity. Buddhist women, even centuries ago, felt the need for an object of spiritual worship that was closer to their own experience than to the world of the male-dominated *sanghas* (Buddhist spiritual communities), which focused on the Buddha and were presided over by a male master or head priest. Even though nuns and monks lived separately, Buddhist nunneries were subordinate within the sanghas. A certain element of spiritual compassion and giving of oneself can perhaps only be represented as female: The devotion to helping others, and the wish to save all beings from danger may be rooted in the maternal instinct. Soon, if a nun became renowned for her enlightenment or spirituality, she would be given the title Kuan Yin to signify that she possessed the qualities of spiritual help associated with the Avalokitesvara bodhisattva; and in the end, it is this female form of Kuan Yin that endured and has come to be worshiped by millions of people today, both men and women.

The original Avalokitesvara serves as a major figure of Tibetan Buddhism, and the Dalai Lama is traditionally understood to be his incarnation on

觀
音

earth, so the masculine form of the Bodhisattva did not disappear entirely. In current practice, the two have become separate entities.

Myths and Legends of Kuan Yin

Around the twelfth century C.E., Buddhist laypeople began to worship Kuan Yin on a wide scale, spreading her cult throughout China. The White Lotus movement, founded by Mao Tzu-yan (ca. 1086–1166), drew in people of Buddhist beliefs who didn't want to fully commit themselves to the vows of the sangha. Combining work and family life with Buddhist devotions, members of the White Lotus movement kept a vegetarian diet and engaged in good deeds, such as printing and distributing sutras, building roads and bridges, and providing drinking water and tea to pilgrims and the homeless. Retaining their married status and interests in the worldly life, they nevertheless founded small, private cloisters, temples, and meditation halls. Kuan Yin worship was a prominent feature of the movement, and some stories about the Bodhisattva of Compassion are derived from that period.

The author Ch'en Chou (1214–1297) tells of one such temple. In 949 C.E. the property had belonged to a wealthy widow named Chang who recited the Lotus

觀
音

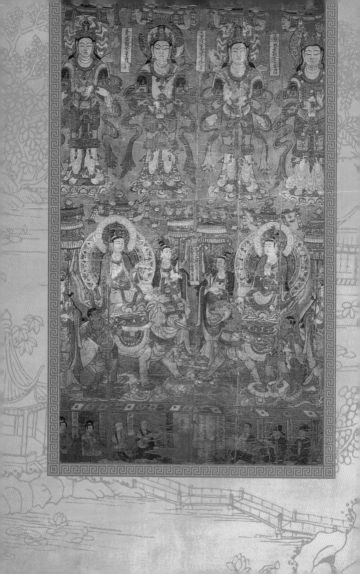

Sutra daily. One night she dreamed that seven monks were born from a lotus flower in the place where she lived. The widow Chang took the monks in her dream to be a direct sign from Kuan Yin, encouraging her to establish a sanctuary in her home. So she donated the house and a considerable amount of her property to a monk with the provision that it be turned into a Kuan Yin temple.

Another story from the period tells that three generations of the same family worshiped at a temple consecrated to the white-robed Kuan Yin and consulted the divination sticks kept there. The family was blessed with a period of uncommon good fortune and, attributing this circumstance to Kuan Yin, donated acres of land to the temple, which grew in influence over the decades.

Women belonging to the White Lotus movement constructed caves as sanctuaries to Kuan Yin. The female worshipers were buried in the caves and at their death took on the religious name of one of her incarnations, Miao-shan, as an epithet to recall their spiritual qualities.

Through these and other personal stories and efforts, the myths and legends of Kuan Yin spread throughout China and later Southeast Asia and Japan. In time, more lay Buddhist movements with Kuan Yin as a central figure sprouted up and helped to spread her fame.

PRINCESS MIAO-SHAN

For generations the Chinese have recounted the
legend of Princess Miao-shan, said to have been a
historical figure who was the very first incarnation
of Kuan Yin. In this well-known tale, Princess Miao-
shan becomes the thousand-armed Kuan Yin, a figure
that is found in temples throughout China and
Southeast Asia and was a descendant of a similar form
of Avalokitesvara.

*Miao-shan was the third daughter of King Miao-
chuang, and her name meant "wonderful adornment."
She was by nature drawn to Buddhism and from an early
age kept a vegetarian diet, read scriptures by day, and
meditated at night. The king had no sons, but he hoped
to choose an heir to his throne from among of his sons-
in-law. When Miao-shan reached marriageable age she
refused to marry, unlike her two obedient sisters who had
married the men their father chose. The king was greatly
angered by Miao-shan's refusal and ordered that she be
punished in various ways. She was first confined to the
back garden and forced to perform hard labor. When,
with the help of the gods, she completed all the arduous
tasks assigned to her, she was allowed to go to the White
Sparrow Nunnery, only to undergo further trials her
father hoped would dissuade her from pursuing the*

spiritual path. The Princess persevered, however, and her father was so furious he burned down the nunnery, killed the 500 nuns inside, and had Miao-shan executed for her unfilial behavior.

While a mountain spirit safeguarded her body, Miao-shan's soul made the rounds of hell and saved beings there by preaching to them. She then returned to the world, went to Hsiang-shan, meditated for nine years, and achieved enlightenment.

By this time, the king had fallen ill with a mysterious disease that had no cure. Miao-shan, disguised as a mendicant monk, came to the palace and told him that there was only one remedy that would save him: a medicine concocted with the eyes and hands of someone who had never felt anger. She then told him where he could find such a person. When the king's messengers arrived, she willingly cut out her own eyes and had her own hands severed. The king recovered his health after taking the miraculous medicine and came with his royal entourage on a pilgrimage to offer thanks to his savior. He recognized the eyeless and handless ascetic as none other than his own daughter. Overwhelmed with remorse, he and the rest of the royal family converted to Buddhism. Miao-shan was then transformed into her true form, the Thousand-eyed and Thousand-armed Kuan Yin.

FISH-BASKET KUAN YIN

This very old legend tells of an apparition of Kuan Yin who converts people to Buddhism, bringing new disciples into the fold like fish into a basket. During the T'ang Dynasty (618–907 C.E.), when Buddhism was very popular in China, the people of the eastern part of the Shensi province loved to hunt and cared little for the principles expounded by the Buddha. In 809, it is said, a beautiful woman appeared one day and said that she would marry any man who could memorize the "Universal Gateway" chapter of the Lotus Sutra.

The next morning twenty men passed the test. Saying that she could not marry them all, she asked them to memorize the Diamond Sutra, another important Buddhist text. More than ten men could recite it by the next morning.

The beautiful young woman then asked them to memorize the entire Lotus Sutra. This time, only Mr. Ma succeeded. He made wedding preparations and sent for the young woman to come to his house. Upon her arrival, she announced that she felt ill and asked to rest in another room. Before the wedding guests had departed, she suddenly died. Her body decomposed very quickly and she had to be buried immediately.

Several days later, an old monk wearing a purple robe asked Mr. Ma to show him the grave site. The monk opened the tomb and touched the body with his staff, revealing to those who had gathered for the strange event that the flesh had fallen away and the dead woman's bones were held together by a golden chain, the manifestation of a great sage who, the monk said, had come to deliver them from evil karma. After washing the bones with water, he wrapped them in a bundle on his staff and ascended to heaven.

Due to this astonishing miracle numerous people converted to Buddhism. Many paintings of *Yu-lan Kuan Yin* ("Kuan Yin with the fish basket") were produced from this period onwards.

KUAN YIN OF THE SOUTH SEA

Kuan Yin's sacred island shrine at Mount P'u-t'o is home to another manifestation of the Bodhisattva. Called *Nan-hai Kuan-yin*, or Kuan Yin of the South Sea, she sits on a rock before a stand of bamboo, behind her the circle of a full moon. She is sometimes depicted carrying a vase of willow branches or standing next to one. A boy and a girl may attend her, and a parrot often hovers above her shoulder carrying a rosary in its beak.

The story associated with Kuan Yin of the South Sea involves her incarnation as princess Miao-shan. When the princess's father burned the nunnery and had his daughter executed, Miao-shan traveled through hell and saved souls by teaching them Buddhism. After her sojourn, the Buddha told her to go to Hsiang-shan, or Fragrant Mountain, close to the South China Sea island of Macau, to practice austerities. The Buddha said that in Hsiang-shan stood a very old temple where the Immortals had lived in retirement in former lives, and there, upon the P'u-t'o rock, she was to practice spiritual cultivation.

Shan-ts'ai, the attendant associated with Kuan Yin, was originally a young pilgrim who visited fifty-three teachers in order to learn the *Buddha Dharma* (the spiritual laws as told by Buddha). Princess Miao-shan, his twenty-eighth teacher, was very impressed with him. In order to test his faith, Miao-shan asked the Earth God to have the Immortals transform themselves into robbers and ruffians and push her down the face of a cliff. Without hesitation, Shan-ts'ai jumped to join her, but as they fell, Miao-shan had him look down at the bottom of the gorge, where he saw his own corpse lying. At that moment he began ascending, in broad daylight, freed from all constraints of his physical body. So the princess made him her permanent attendant to

reward him for the blind faith he had shown her, and
since then he has been associated with Kuan Yin.

The attendant young girl was the daughter of the
Dragon King whose palace Kuan Yin had visited to
teach a *dharani* (a protective spell) found in the Lotus
Sutra. In gratitude, the King's daughter wished to
bestow Kuan Yin with a night-illuminating pearl, so
that she could read sutras at night. The granddaughter
of the Dragon King offered to take the precious pearl
to Kuan Yin and asked to become the Bodhisattva's
disciple.

TALES OF KUAN YIN'S MIRACLES

In his book on Kuan Yin, *Bodhisattva of Compassion*,[4]
John Blofeld tells the story of a novice nun who had
been vowed to Buddhist service at the time of her
elder brother's illness. The young man was on the
point of death, and the family's doctor had declared
that there was no hope of saving him. His aunt sent
the doctor away and called all the neighbors and
family members to gather around and recite a dharani
from the Lotus Sutra for his protection. Toward
midnight, the brother, who had been lying in a coma,
woke up and shouted, "Look at that girl!" Several
people saw sitting on the rafters of the house a young
woman in flowing robes who looked like Princess
Miao-shan. They all heard the girl laugh. In her hand

was a vase—the traditional vessel in which Kuan Yin stores the Dew of Compassion—which she tipped so that some of the liquid fell on the brother's head. The apparition vanished in a flash, and everyone marveled at what had happened. The aunt declared that there was no need for further recitation and told everyone to go home. Within two days, the brother had completely recovered, and his younger sister began her service at a Buddhist nunnery.[5]

KANNON: THE JAPANESE KUAN YIN

In Japan, Kuan Yin is known as Kannon. One well-known legend tells of an aristocratic young girl, Chujo Hime, who as a child became famous in her village for her love and protection of those in need and animals. Her stepmother, however, treated her badly and even tried to kill her. The young girl took refuge in Mount Hibari, and her father searched for two years before he managed to find her. To protect her from his ill-intentioned wife, he had arranged for Chujo Hime's marriage to the emperor of Japan. When he told his daughter of the plan, she turned the offer down, for she had made vows to the Buddha to remain single all her life and to devote herself to the salvation of all beings. Despite her father's anger and sadness, Chujo Hime entered the Taima-deva

Convent in the province of Yamato, and there each day supplicated Amitabha Buddha, the Lord of the Pure Land, and perhaps the most popular buddha in China, to grant her plea for the salvation of all beings.

One day, an elderly man knocked at her cell door and said he would show her Amitabha Buddha's Western Paradise if she carried out some unusual instructions. She was told to gather one hundred lotus stalks and place them in a well that had miraculously appeared in the courtyard of the nunnery. As soon as the stalks came in contact with the well water, they turned brilliant colors in all the shades of the rainbow. Shortly afterward, a young woman appeared out of nowhere with a loom on which for six uninterrupted hours she wove a tapestry depicting Buddha's Pure Land. Yet another miracle occurred when the weaving was complete, for the tapestry was revealed to be much larger than the room that contained the loom. Deeply moved by all the miraculous events, Chujo Hime bowed her head, and the elderly man and the young woman instantly transformed themselves into Amitabha, the Buddha of the Western Paradise, and Kannon.

觀
音

The Sacred Island of P'u-t'o

P'u-t'o Island, in Chekiang, China, is considered the spiritual home of Kuan Yin, and it is here that she made her all-powerful vow, before Amitabha Buddha and many other buddhas, to postpone her reward for the sake of those yet to be enlightened. The site was one of the three major sacred places where great bodhisattvas manifested themselves in human form and where pilgrims and worshipers could hope to receive blessings and answers to their prayers. P'u-t'o became the most important shrine to Kuan Yin quite late, reaching its peak only after the eighteenth century.

觀
音

One of the many islands forming the Chou-shan Archipelago in the East China Sea, P'u-t'o extends about 8 1/2 miles from north to south, and 3 1/2 miles from east to west. The island is strategically placed along a sea-lane connecting China and Japan. Hilly, lush, and dotted with low-lying mountains and haunting rock formations, it seems the perfect surroundings for a bodhisattva.

The earliest recorded sightings of Kuan Yin at P'u-t'o were reported by royal emissaries traversing the passage

on ships, who found themselves in life-endangering situations and were saved by her. Soon, miracles of shipwreck rescues became the legend of the island, and Buddhists began to make pilgrimages in hopes of seeing an apparition of Kuan Yin.

Over the centuries famous voyagers and ordinary pilgrims alike traveled to the island in search of blessings from Kuan Yin, and the practice continues to be extremely popular. The visitors left material contributions that helped build up the island as a sacred pilgrimage site, constructed temples, and adapted natural sanctuaries where one can retire for meditation. Tourists from mainland China, Taiwan, Hong Kong, and the Philippines come to vacation here and hope to be touched by the blessings of the Bodhisattva.

觀
音

Building Your Own
Kuan Yin Altar

Short of going on a pilgrimage to the island of
P'u-t'o or visiting one of her temples in the United
States, the best way to seek Kuan Yin's blessing is to
build an altar to her in your home or garden.

Choose a place that is quiet and set apart from the
everyday activities of the household. It may be a corner
of your bedroom, or a windowsill, or you can make an
altar within a box you decorate especially for her. If
her shrine is in a garden, choose a grotto or cavelike
spot, perhaps beneath a tree or in a corner by a garden
wall. The altar should be in a spot where you will be
able to sit and meditate and allow Kuan Yin's energy
to pervade you.

The figurine in your *Kuan Yin* box should be the
centerpiece of your shrine, and you may wish to
follow the tradition of Pure Land Buddhist temples
dedicated to the Bodhisattva, where censers release
clouds of scented smoke before altars bedecked with
a profusion of flowers and candles.

Before beginning worship and rituals to Kuan Yin,
Pure Land monks, nuns, and lay devotees purify

觀
音

themselves with ablutions, but also with a period of silent contemplation to banish worldly thoughts extraneous to the rite.

Keep your altar beautifully tidy and fresh, like a true abode for the Bodhisattva. This is the place of her worship; this is the place of vision and guidance.

觀音

Rituals and Worship

The focus of meditation for Pure Land devotees of Kuan Yin is Pure Mind, a state of consciousness unencumbered by all illusions. It is thought that a sacred being, such as the Bodhisattva, can serve as an immensely powerful visualization tool to help us enter into the state of Pure Mind.

Enlightenment and final liberation from suffering are attained by transcending all ego illusions. Powerful Buddhist techniques help us approach a state of meditation in which the mind is turned back upon itself—it literally becomes a pure mirror—and all illusions are reflected as such, proving that they have no real existence except as figments of our mental activity. Once the truth is discovered, one can live in the Ultimate Reality, thus realizing enlightenment.

In this section you will find a few meditations and rituals for worshiping Kuan Yin, but if you want to discover more or are unfamiliar with meditation, go to one of Kuan Yin's many temples and talk to a monk or nun. He or she will give you expert advice

觀
音

on devotions for beginners, and may recommend
meditation sessions you can join to learn more. Once
you experience the correct frame of mind, you can
carry it over into your own private meditations.

CALLING KUAN YIN

The high point of all Kuan Yin meditations is the
invocation of her name, a practice that is never omitted
from any Pure Land traditional practice dedicated
to her. Begin chanting *Namo Kuan Shih Yin P'u-Sa*
(Hail to Kuan Shih Yin Bodhisattva) over and over
again at a slow tempo that is gradually quickened. This
chant works as a mantra: It brings quiet to the mind
and spirit and helps to break the thought patterns that
screen silence from our perception.

In Pure Land temples, nuns, monks, recluses, and
ordinary laypeople gather together in the meditation
hall, and after a period of silence the chanting is begun
by the chiming of a sacred instrument. Walking
around the altar clockwise in single file, the devotees
circulate through the hall chanting Kuan Yin's name
with gathering momentum. Growing quicker and
louder, the chant is after a while interrupted by
another loud chime, and everyone returns to the
meditation position.

The silence after this meditation is deeper than it

was during the first period. The more you practice the meditation, the deeper the silence and the more transparent Ultimate Reality will become. Try to meditate every day at the same time for a period of at least a week; whether in the morning or evening, attempt to dedicate at least 20 minutes to this practice and you will feel calmer, touched by the radiance of the Bodhisattva.

KUAN YIN VISUALIZATION

In the *Bodhisattva of Compassion*, Blofeld tells of a Pure Land Buddhist nun he met in Canton. The nun had not been content with merely reciting Kuan Yin's name during her meditations; she wished to *see* her, and under the guidance of a monk at the monastery where she resided, she learned a new meditation, more yogic than that of the Pure Land tradition, which is paraphrased here.

Sit quietly and take a few slow, deep breaths, while you make your mind empty. Tell yourself that there is nothing there. With your inner vision you confirm that there is nothing there, just quiet, velvety darkness.

Slowly, see that the moon has risen out of the sea of darkness, and see it as full and white, floating above the sea. Stare at it with your inner vision and feel calmed by it, happy and secure. Then the moon

becomes smaller and smaller until it becomes a pearl, so bright it almost hurts to look at. Next, the pearl starts to grow again and you see that it is Kuan Yin, gleaming white, standing against the backdrop of the sky, dressed in white floating robes, her feet resting on a lotus that floats on the waves of the dark ocean. You must concentrate until you see her with full clarity, and you will see that she is smiling a radiant smile at you, and she is so happy to see you that tears begin to glisten in her gentle, dark eyes.

If you whisper her name gently and remain very calm, holding your mind very still and focused on Kuan Yin, you will be able to see her for a very long time. When she departs, she gets smaller and smaller, until you can no longer see her floating on the ocean. Then you will notice that the night sky and the ocean have disappeared too. There is only pure space left: Nothingness. Quiet, gentle space that goes on forever. The space stays and stays in your mind until "you" disappear and there is only space left. That is the true you. Nothing. Void. The space that exists between one breath and another.

This very powerful meditation on Kuan Yin becomes stronger the more you practice it. Return to your daily activities only after resting for a few minutes after the meditation.

觀
音

Kuan Yin Sutras

Author Chun-Fang Yu, one of the world's leading authorities on Kuan Yin, went to Hangzhou, the capital of Chekiang province in eastern China, during the spring pilgrimage season a few years ago. Large groups of women arrived every day to pay their respects to Kuan Yin at the Upper T'ien-chu Temple. The songs they sang about the Bodhisattva were called "Kuan-yin ching," or Kuan Yin Sutra. She has translated some of them into English:

觀
音

> South Sea Temple, Purple Bamboo Grove.
> Kuan Yin emerges from Purple Bamboo Grove.
> A daughter-in-law from the ends of the earth
>   worships Kuan Yin.
> Having been worshiped, Kuan Yin appears
>   in front of my eyes.
> A thousand good roads lead to Rocky Mountain.
> Adoration of Kuan Shih Yin,
>   the Great Compassionate One.[6]

When the spring breeze blows and the water is clear.
I must go to Hangchow to worship Kuan Yin.
Look at the high mountain with a thousand buddhas,
Look at the West Lake with the limpid water.
The West Lake has bridges spanning fifteen
    and sixteen li.
The West Lake faces the Ling-yin Temple.
And the Ling-yin Temple faces
    the Fragrant Water Bridge.
Willow trees alternate with peach trees.
Granny Kuan Yin lives in the mountain creek
    of nine winding paths.
I came bearing incense from another county,
    from another province.
Adoration to the Buddha, Amitabha.[7]

Reading the two sutras above may inspire you to
write your own Kuan Yin song, as the experience of
your Kuan Yin meditations gives you words to express
your gratitude to the Bodhisattva.

The most commonly recited sutra associated with
Kuan Yin is the "Universal Gateway" chapter of the
Lotus Sutra. It tells of the vow that the Buddha
asked Kuan Yin to swear before she could be called
the Bodhisattva of Compassion. Every would-be
bodhisattva must take the bodhisattva vow, often

recited as a dharani. In this retelling of the sacred
text, one of Buddha's other bodhisattvas attending
the ceremony asked Buddha how Kuan Yin came to
be known as Bodhisattva of Infinite Compassion:

> World Honored One,
> Complete with Wondrous Hallmarks,
> Several questions I would ask again.
> How did this disciple of the Buddha,
> Earn the name Kuan Yin?

Then the World Honored One answered in
melodious verse to his questioner, Bodhisattva
Infinite Resolve:

> Come listen and I'll tell you Kuan Yin's story
> How deftly she responds to every side;
> Spanning ages past the ken of numbers,
> With oceanic vows both deep and wide.

> Serving ancient Buddhas, several billions,
> Her pure and lofty vows in brief I'll tell.
> Whoever sees her face or learns about her,
> Who can hold this Bodhisattva's name,
> Will leave behind the sorrows of existence,
> And so this cultivation's not in vain!

觀
音

Should you be pushed into a raging fire,
By enemies so harmful, mean, and cruel,
Evoke the strength of Kuan Yin Bodhisattva
The blaze will turn into a limpid pool.

If cast adrift upon the mighty ocean,
Where dragons, ghosts, and sharks in turn surround,
Evoke the strength of Kuan Yin Bodhisattva,
You'll float atop the waves and will not drown.

Suppose an evil person pushed you headlong,
From atop the peak called Wondrous Tall,
Evoke the strength of Kuan Yin Bodhisattva,
And like the sun in space you will not fall.

Perhaps you tumble down from Vajra Mountain,
Fleeing wicked ruffians who pursue,
Evoke the strength of Kuan Yin Bodhisattva,
And not the slightest harm will come to you.

Surrounded by a mob of heartless bandits,
Their weapons drawn, with murder on their minds,
Evoke the strength of Kuan Yin Bodhisattva,
Their evil hearts will soften and turn kind.

觀
音

If you are on the verge of execution,
Sentenced by the State, condemned to die,
Evoke the strength of Kuan Yin Bodhisattva,
The sword will break to pieces just in time.

If bound and chained, restrained by ropes and shackles,
With hands and feet confined in stocks and gyres,
Evoke the strength of Kuan Yin Bodhisattva,
The fetters by themselves will fall aside.

Hexes, poison, magic spells, and voodoo,
Cast by those who plot to do you in,
Return to curse the sorcerer who sent them,
When you invoke the power of Kuan Yin.

If you meet with evil Rakshashas,
Lethal dragons, ghosts, and vicious beasts,
Evoke the strength of Kuan Yin Bodhisattva,
None will dare to harm you in the least.

Circled round and trapped by savage creatures,
With razor fangs and claws that terrify,
Evoke the strength of Kuan Yin Bodhisattva,
And they will quickly flee to every side.

Facing vipers, scorpions, and pythons,
Belching poisons, fumes, and scorching flames,
Evoke the strength of Kuan Yin Bodhisattva,
They'll shrink and turn away before his name.

When thunderclouds explode and lightning crackles,
Dumping sleet, and hail, and heavy rains,
Evoke the strength of Kuan Yin Bodhisattva,
The skies will clear, the storms will drift away.

Living beings harassed and vexed, and troubled,
By countless sorrows, burdened without cease,
This Bodhisattva's wondrous wisdom-power.
Can help the suffering world obtain relief.

Perfect and complete in psychic power,
Widely versed in wisdom's subtle skills,
In lands throughout the ten directions,
The Bodhisattva manifests at will.

The agony amid the Evil Pathways,
The torments of the ghosts, the beasts, the hells,
The pains of birth, the aged, sick, and dying,
The Bodhisattva gradually dispels.

O Thou of true regard, of pure regard,
Regard far-reaching, wise, and truly great,
Thy loving-kindness, sympathy, and deep regard,
I vow to ever laud and venerate.

Your wisdom-sun can break apart the darkness,
Immaculate, your virgin light unfurls,
To quell disasters, winds, and storms, and fires,
A universal light for all the world.

Wellspring of compassion, precepts' thunder,
Your wondrous cloud of kindness covers all.
Extinguishing the fires of life's afflictions,
As the rain of sweet-dew Dharma falls.

In trials, suits, and civil confrontations,
When fear runs high, when warring armies near,
Evoke the strength of Kuan Yin Bodhisattva,
Vengeance and bad feelings disappear.

Fine and wondrous sound: Kuan Yin!
Brahma-sound, steady as the tides.
A name transcending every worldly sound,
Kuan Yin! Stay forever in my mind.

觀
音

Let not a single doubt arise to haunt us,
For Kuan Yin Bodhisattva, Holy Goddess,
Amid life's troubles, and the pains of dying,
Will ever be our refuge, and our aid.
O Holy One! Replete with every virtue,
Your kindly gaze beholds all living beings.
A boundless sea you are, of every blessing.
And let us bow to offer our esteem![8]

Then the Bodhisattva Guardian of the Earth arose from his seat, went before the Buddha and exclaimed, "O World-Honored One, living beings must have abundant merit and virtue to hear this chapter on Kuan Yin Bodhisattva's sovereign deeds, and how she [referring to 'he,' as expressed above] universally responds with spiritual power."

These verses are composed of sacred words recited in ceremonies during the religious festivals in honor of Kuan Yin, which fall on the nineteenth day of the second, sixth, and ninth lunar months.

INVOCATION OF KUAN YIN

Should you feel you are in danger or find yourself in an uncomfortable situation in which you feel powerless and want to invoke the power of Kuan Yin quickly, say the following words:

I call upon the Bodhisattva who sees and hears the sufferings of the world.

This invocation has been used throughout the centuries to call on Kuan Yin's powers. You can also use the phrase to call Kuan Yin at the beginning of your meditations: Repeat it several times for a number of minutes, like a mantra, until you feel your whole body relax, your breath and heartbeat slow down, and your mind begin to empty.

Kuan Yin is a very powerful Bodhisattva who will always come to your rescue. Millions of people throughout the Buddhist world attest to her very real power of compassion. May she bless your life as well!

觀
音

Notes to the Text

[1] Soothill, W. E. *The Lotus of the Wonderful Law*.
Oxford: Clarendon Press, 1930.

[2] Karashima Seishi. *The Textural Study of the
Chinese Versions of the Saddharmapundarika Sutra
in Light of the Sanskrit and Tibetan Version*. Tokyo:
Sankino, 1992.

[3] Chung-Fang Yu. *Kuan Yin*. New York: Columbia
University Press, 2001.

[4] Blofeld, John. *Bodhisattva of Compassion*. Boston:
Shambhala Editions, 1977.

[5] —. Ibid.

[6] Chung-Fang Yu. *Kuan Yin*. New York: Columbia
University Press, 2001.

[7] —. Ibid.

[8] Translated from Sanskrit into Chinese by
Tripitaka Dharma Master Kumarajiva of the Yao
Chin Dynasty. Translated from Chinese into
English by the Buddhist Translation Society,
Dharma Realm Buddhist University, Ukiah,
California.

觀
音

further Reading

Blofeld, John. *Bodhisattva of Compassion*. Boston: Shambhala Editions, 1977.

Boucher, Sandy. *Discovering Kuan Yin*. Boston: Beacon Press, 1999.

Chung-Fang Yu. *Kuan Yin*. New York: Columbia University Press, 2001.

Palmer, Martin and Jay Ramsay. *Kuan Yin, Myths and Prophecies of the Chinese Goddess of Compassion*. London: Thorsons, HarperCollins, 1995.

Reis-Habito, Maria. "The Bodhisattva Guanyin and the Virgin Mary" in *Christian Studies*, 13. University of Hawaii Press, 1993.

觀
音

Art Acknowledgments

BOOK COVER: *Seated Kuan Yin*, He Chaozong, Xiemen Museum, Fujian, China.

ENDPAPERS: *Chinese Landscape*, British Museum, London.

PAGE 2: *Seated Kuan Yin*, Nelson-Atkins Museum of Art, Kansas City.

PAGE 5: *Seated Kuan Yin*, He Chaozong, Xiemen Museum, Fujian, China.

PAGE 6: *Kuan Yin seated on a Fu Dog with Scepter*, private collection.

PAGE 8: BACKGROUND *The Eight Immortals*, Asian Art Museum, San Francisco. FIGURINE *Seated Kuan Yin*, He Chaozong, Xiemen Museum, Fujian, China.

PAGE 10: *Seated Kuan Yin*, He Chaozong, Xiemen Museum, Fujian, China.

PAGE 11: *Kuan Yin on an Elephant*, private collection.

PAGE 12: *Four-Armed Kuan Yin and Companions*, Cultural Relics Publishing House, Beijing, China.

93

觀
音